Passive Income Ideas

----- ✌🏻🌿 -----

Top Streams Of Income To Make Money While You Sleep And Achieve Financial Freedom

By Logan King

© Copyright 2017 - All rights reserved.

The contents of this book may not be reproduced, duplicated or transmitted without direct written permission from the author.

Under no circumstances will any legal responsibility or blame be held against the publisher for any reparation, damages, or monetary loss due to the information herein, either directly or indirectly.

Legal Notice:

This book is copyright protected. This is only for personal use. You cannot amend, distribute, sell, use, quote or paraphrase any part or the content within this book without the consent of the author.

Disclaimer Notice:

Please note the information contained within this document is for educational and entertainment purposes only. Every attempt has been made to provide accurate, up to date and reliable complete information. No warranties of any kind are expressed or implied. Readers acknowledge that the author is not engaging in the rendering of legal, financial, medical or professional advice. The content of this book has been derived from various sources. Please consult a licensed professional before attempting any techniques outlined in this book.

By reading this document, the reader agrees that under no circumstances are is the author responsible for any losses, direct or indirect, which are incurred as a result of the use of information contained within this document, including, but not limited to, — errors, omissions, or inaccuracies.

Table Of Contents

Introduction 4

Chapter One: Upgrade Your Thinking 6

Chapter Two: The Potential Of Online Money 10

Chapter Three: Selling Shirt Designs 18

Chapter Four: Ebook Publishing 23

Chapter Five: Becoming An Affiliate 31

Chapter Six: Grow Into A Youtube Icon 37

Chapter Seven: More Passive Income Avenues 41

Conclusion 46

Introduction

Welcome, and let me congratulate you on taking this step on your journey to learning more about passive income and how it can vastly improve our lives!

In the current state of affairs, if you aren't willing to shift your mindset and take chances, you are sure to fall behind the pack. It is easy for us to look at something that we know nothing about and that is relatively new and assume it is a fad and likely to die soon. It is also easy for us to jump into a venture blind with high hopes of riches and leave scarred.

Lucky neither of these describes the universe that is the Internet. The longer the Internet stays around, the more we use it and turn it into an important part of our daily lives. It's already close to impossible to live without it! And sure, the Internet may have had a period in its very young stages where people lost money with no direction and following unproven trends, but most of those kinks have been ironed out since!

We now can find so many Internet business trajectories demonstrating high rates of success and monetary return that it would be completely foolish to overlook this new avenue of possibilities!

If you have the courage to start a business, that task becomes exponentially easier on the Internet with the vastly reduced overhead. And even if you don't want to shoot that high with a entire business and just want to make a few consistent bucks in the background, there are countless methods for that as well.

The bottom line is that if you aren't at least CONSIDERING how you can jack into the Internet to receive passive income, you are limiting what your life could be and you're leaving money on the table for others to scoop up!

Chapter One:

Upgrade Your Thinking

Our thinking is so automatic that we sometimes cannot even fathom that it is our barrier to success.

The Skeptic

In the pursuit of comfort and least risk, we end up not jumping at the blinking opportunities right in front of our faces! We might tell ourselves, "There must be a catch." or "It has to be a scam and people making money are fake stories or one in a million."

The thing is, it's to the benefit of all online entrepreneurs to let people continue to stay in the dark with these blinders on, so less competition enters the online marketplace! If this is you, I urge you to shift your assumptions about the Internet and what it can offer.

You may even be asking, if these secrets are so valuable, why would I be giving them out? Why invite others to join the arena and take a piece of my pie away? Again, that is the mindset that needs to be dropped! It is to everyone's benefit when people evolve and adopt new technology. I believe that prosperity is not a zero sum game where your input takes away from my earnings. Instead, we can all provide value and open up pathways for others to also join in on the parade!

We are in the most amazing period of time and no matter the temporary swings in the stock market and economy, things eventually go back towards an upward trend of improvement. To think otherwise is to put yourself in a mindset of scarcity where the world is bleak and money is always of reach, especially passive income.

On the subject of mindset: incredible research and anecdotes have shown the power of our thinking and how it manifests into what we acquire and become. Whether you are convinced the law of attraction is real or spiritual hullabaloo, the core concept is clear as can be. You follow the path towards passive income online with passion and you will start to identify with the results. Good milestones along the way can be absorbed since it aligns with your goal and roadblocks don't affect you deeply because negativity becomes foreign to you.

Of course this doesn't mean you start to become delusional, or ignore it if your life starts falling apart. It means you simply stop taking hits to the ego so personally.

Is Failure Inevitable?

Who is your favorite athlete?

Who is your favorite comedian?

Who is your entrepreneur?

Now close your eyes and think about each of those people for a few seconds.

Chapter One: Upgrade Your Thinking

I'd wager that what you thought about were the greatest moments in their lives. Maybe you remember seeing them in person, while you gazed in awe of such a powerful and successful person. Maybe you wondered for a moment what it was that stood between you, what force placed them at the top while you stagnated below.

The truth is that this is the highlight reel. Sure it is inspiring and gives us a good boost of motivation to see what can be done, but it ignores the failure behind the trophies or accolades. It's natural for friends and family to want to protect you from high risk situations, but with that care they end up being friction against your desire for what they don't have.

Michael Jordan wasn't shooting basketballs or wowing the crowds the moment he exited his mother's womb! He had to try, fail, pick himself up, and fail again until his persistence manifested into the legend we all know. He was even cut from his high school basketball team! It is massively important to hold your own standards in the face of rejection. Even with that devastating cut to the high school team, his passion remained unwavered.

Stephen King books can be found in every bookstore across America and likely throughout the world! But was he a similar story to Michael Jordan or a prodigy from birth? I think you know the answer!

One of his first completed manuscripts was *Carrie* and was rejected by dozens of publishers... DOZENS! And even with that many rejections, he kept on submitting his work, at one point tossing his novel in the trash, and ended up getting the deal of a lifetime! Now Stephen King is a household name that commands respect. Rejection might be one of the most painful experiences we can have, but it's also a test of our strength.

How do we respond to the stress put in front of us? Do we choose to cave in and accept our loss personally or push on towards to the larger goal?

Here's one more example if those two didn't hit home enough for you. The first time Jerry Seinfeld went on stage to do a comedy act, did he kill it and immediately land his own show that would span across multiple seasons? Quite the opposite! He tensed up in fear, and could barely tell his first jokes ever. The crowd even booed him off stage for his embarrassing display of the art of comedy. But like all successful people, he took that as a challenge and came back again and again until his personality could shine through. Soon, through his struggles in the brutal world of stand up comedy, doors ended up opening for him that once were deemed ludicrous.

Chapter Two:

The Potential Of Online Money

Imagine having your own robot to handle your business. Or having a product in a niche that competitors are too lazy to go after.

To me, this encapsulates the concept of the current state of the Internet. Some would argue that the Internet is still in its infancy stages, but I would say it's more like a toddler at this point. More and more people are catching on to the trends and revolutionary ways to communicate and transact, but it isn't even close to being one hundred percent of the population.

Surely you have friends or family that think there is very little money to be made on the Internet. That the sites they visit to read news or entertainment are lucky or have some hidden ways they're making money. It seems like in their eyes that you are either making zero dollars or have a completely set up online business that popped up out of thin air.

However, it's this middle ground where the gold is. My question to people who like to doubt online money is, "What amount per week or per month would you consider to be worth pursuing? And what if it was passive income?" The answer that should arise is any amount. Passive income is a totally foreign concept to the people uneducated in the economy of the Internet. Usually passive income is only relegated in people's minds as dividends on your investments, but I would argue that not even that is passive income. And even worse, when people are shown proof of the money made online by an Average Joe, the skeptic still thinks, "Wow that's impressive, but I can't do that."

They need to realize what the Internet can offer with its unique digital format. If I make a physical toy train and sell it physically to someone else, great! But now I need the resources to make another toy train for the next possible customer. Each customer wants their own 'fresh' product.

However, thanks to the Internet, we can go the route of digital products! In this scenario I make a PDF or guide based on my knowledge and sell it online. One person buys it, great! But that person didn't take the file away from me. It was merely cloned, if you will, and I am all set to sell it again without needing additional resources!

This is only one example of the core concept of making passive income online, but shows the slight tweak in thinking that's required for this arena.

Your Online Storefront

Not only are the opportunities there, but the costs to play the Internet money game are cheaper than you expect! I get asked the question why I would bother with online money with the possibility of achieving the 'myth' of passive income, but the real question is why would you bother with a real physical business.

Chapter Two: The Potential Of Online Money

The current state of the economy makes it harder and harder to start your own business and comply with all the regulations that seem to pile on top of each other. You need to acquire the land to set up your store, get the inventory ahead of time, hope it all sells... I hope you have a couple grand to toss up for a business that has no promise of doing well enough to make your investment back!

It depends on your state of residence, but the hassles of regulations can really keep a vice on your neck after risking so much with your initial investment! There are even stories of successful restaurants in major metropolitan cities that have to close down. The fines from mostly outdated infractions keep breathing room extremely limited.

The only digital 'real estate' you arguably need is a domain name. Beyond that, the online world is your oyster.

You are not required to set up bathrooms on your website or risk being fined. You are not required to maintain a functioning carbon monoxide detector.

In essence, it's business stripped to its bare bones. It is the sandbox that is getting more of the attention of the bigger kids, but is still large enough for everyone to have a significant spot.

The Legitimate Concern

Let's give the Debbie Downers one 'win' even though it still doesn't hold a strong case against pursuing passive income.

Sure, you won't be making xyz money per hour the second you enter the online arena, so on the surface it looks like you are working for no compensation or wasting your time. But that is the mindset of those who cannot think of building up for the future. Work needs to be put in upfront, and once the eyeballs start to look in your direction, they never turn away.

This is the angle that turns most people off. But, I assure you that simply pushing past this roadblock is the hardest step of the passive income journey. It may sometimes feel like you're running through a pitch-black room with only a general sense of which direction leads to the exit, trusting those that gave advice on which way to go and how to go about it.

But this is where your true character shines. Just like I previously mentioned, Michael Jordan and Jerry Seinfeld had to push past rough beginnings, which may have been ammo that their family and friends used against them. There needs to be a brutal but also honest sense of tunnel vision, and always be willing to learn more and ask for help from others.

To the hater's credit, there will be moments of feeling lost. Highs and lows infiltrate all endeavors but the reward for your investment online is worth it every time. Even if everything went south and for some reason the Internet ceased to exist or was banned by the government, the business lessons you'll receive are priceless. So even the worst case scenario shows an overall life improvement from jumping into the online waters.

Trading Time For Money

This is the automatic thought process of 'getting a job.' You get paid by the hour the moment you get hired as an employee. To the outsider, this is why the Internet is a lost cause for a money source. Where are the online cubicles? Where do you sign up for an interview to work for a website?

The concept is simply out of the scope of most folks that merely give it a quick glance.

Chapter Two: The Potential Of Online Money

Like I mentioned above, you will initially be trading time for NO money when you start getting traction on your entrepreneurism wheels. That is the nature of the online marketplace. A newly bought domain with a crude website won't fly to the first page of Google the next day. It needs to be slowly beefed up, like you might expect.

But once you touch a certain threshold, the prior work that you did for 'free' will start to gain attention and make your investment back. It's at this moment that your work has the potential to stack. Older work will be making you money and future work that follows the same success guidelines will likely follow suit. The limit ends up resting solely in your hands!

For me, the most exciting part of this journey is letting something sit alone once you get it going. Maybe hire a few assistants to either hold light maintenance or to grow it further with your instruction. Then, the young-hearted question enters into your mind, what can I do now that I have a moneymaking machine behind me?

Maybe go after those passions that you always held onto in the back of your mind! Or jump into another niche online to continue to provide value!

Certainly in the current volatile economy we exist in, living financially free is far from the realistic goal that comes to mind for most people. Usually the worry is the loss of a job, anticipating a layoff, or surviving until next week on a shrinking paycheck. It's definitely understandable thinking, but how could that mindset ever work towards the dream of passive income? You cement your reality for the worse, and end up making incredibly hard to burst through that train of negative thinking!

Masterminding

It's because of these pitfalls of mental resilience that finding strong-minded people is so critical for you to advance. The easy way out of any rocky road is to say "Yes, I was wrong and should settle for less." But what story or person you admire has followed that way of thinking and found massive success?

The majority of people online that have made money are more than willing to share that knowledge. Usually at a price, and that depends on your budget, but there are even free communities that can provide immense insight. Facebook has groups for any avenue of online entrepreneurship where people are heavily invested in helping each other find their footing. Whether by forums or Twitter lists, you can enter the group of your choosing on the platform of your choosing!

Use the power of the Internet to stay focused and make money through the power of the Internet!

Through these mentors and groups, you will see that the journey doesn't have to be a lonely one. It can if you truly want it to be, but why make things harder on yourself? The instant thought of most things online being a scam starts to loose its grip on your mind when you start to interact with these groups.

You get to see new people or people with just a hair more of experience than you and their results. Unless all the people sharing knowledge are lying to sell a success product with false testimonials, you will be fine. I have come across one in all my years in mastermind groups, and they get ousted quite quickly after lacking proof for their claims and not knowing answers to basic questions.

Chapter Two: The Potential Of Online Money

Let's say you end up joining a few dozen accounts that provide ebook publishing advice on Twitter, a publisher forum, and a couple ebook publishing Facebook groups. With all that support and positivity circling you, how can you not be motivated to succeed? You don't need to only rely on yourself to escape from self-doubting ruts. There are certainly at least a few people that can relate to the exact troubles you're experiencing!

Delegating The Skilled Work

One major turn off is the assumption that you need to know the intricacies of coding and how to create your own website from scratch. The Internet wouldn't benefit from this exclusion of a potential value provider or customer!

Applications and software are rapidly designed to aid the inexperienced to streamline their comfort into the online universe. It's to everyone's benefit that people are brought in online to join in the economic and social revolution.

In reality, you can move into your journey for online passive income with close to no skills at all!

A core concept of scaling up and leveraging your time is learning about the world of delegation. You need to ask yourself, "Is this a tedious task? Is my time better spent on the larger aspects of my business?" It's totally fine to do that work yourself to make sure it is done to your standards and completed promptly. Also, it's entirely reasonable to want to not pay for someone else to help because you are starting out and want to keep expenses low.

But if you have the capital to invest, there is no better method to scale up fast than delegating your tasks. You can write your own ebook and make your own designs, or your can hire someone to worry about that process on your behalf. Maybe you hire five writers at once while you write your own ebook. In a couple weeks you now have six books in the span that you took to create one!

Delegation sounds almost too good to be true, especially in the pursuit of passive income. The only pitfall is that you need to know FOR SURE what to delegate.

You can delegate anything.

As long as the freelancer is getting paid for it, they don't question if the product will be profitable for you. They only worry about giving you the work that you've requested. In the end, they have no stake in your success and are only doing EXACTLY what you want.

You could hire twenty freelancers at once to each make shirt designs with a chair on it. A week later you have twenty designs that you own that you can put up on the online marketplace. Great! Or is it?

In this situation you've likely spent a couple hundred dollars, which is normal, if you hire that many freelancers at once. But was it wisely spent? How many people are searching for shirts with chairs on them? You're the final gate of approval for any product before creation. After the freelancer creates the requested product and you decide that the market is not viable, you are unlikely to get any sort of refund or compensation for a mistake on YOUR part.

Chapter Three:

Selling Shirt Designs

This chapter could have been called 'Selling Shirts' but I believe there's a large separation between the two phrases.

When you think about selling shirts you think about making the art to put on the shirt and then having that printed onto multiple shirts that you might store personally before a purchase. And this is directly in contrast to the concept of passive income. In essence you need to buy the shirt to sell it for EACH sale. You need awareness for every purchase to have stock and deliver it promptly.

Instead, we want to leverage our time and work. There are multiple sites that offer the capability to print and ship the shirt for you! Not only that but they also take care of the small issues that may arise, like refunds and customer service.

The focus is very clear for the online warrior, to provide the best quality designs for these websites that will sell well. They take a cut of the sale for the manufacturing and shipping etc. and you take the rest! It's a venue where you basically sell your creativity to as many people as possible. The art you provide is printed on the shirt and sent out, 'cloning' your work for each sale with no further effort on your part!

This can also be considered drop shipping by most definitions but I find the shirt design route to be the most quick and simple to jump into. Surely you have a favorite YouTuber or social media personality that sells shirts in intervals. They are most likely using this method, granted their marketing and artwork is completely based in their brand and persona, so there isn't as much urgency to be unique and grab stranger's attention.

Amazon has a great program for this avenue called 'Merch By Amazon' but there are many others you can look into, so you can see which is the most competitive for their design providers.

Getting Noticed

I mentioned that large online personalities don't need to market very heavily and I am assuming you are in the opposite situation! The question is, "How do I get eyeballs on my designs?"

It might be a cakewalk for someone who has already walked through the Internet and gained a following to release a product and get instant sales. But we need to be a bit more savvy. Not incredibly more! Just more SMART savvy.

The biggest thing is the market research.

Are there people buying that style of shirt?

What can you do to make it one of a kind?

Is the market over saturated with designs?

Chapter Three: Selling Shirt Designs

You can get the help of others to really dig down but all you need to do is look into the ideas that pop into your head. Once you have a portal you are planning to sell on, you can do your research there. For instance, you can go to Amazon and search with a filter on clothes or shirts with your topic or keyword and see the results.

If there are one hundred plus PAGES of results, you can be sure that your design will have the same chance of getting sales as hitting the lottery! I made the same newbie mistake when I was using the shirt passive income strategy to make an American election shirt, a few months before Election day.

Looking back, that was close to the worst market I could have entered. There were indeed hundreds of pages of designs and my design would have to be close to a Renaissance painter's level of quality to even get a few sales. Your metric needs to not only be that there are shirts under that topic but also, and equally as important, the topic needs to have a reasonable number of listed results.

I like to keep the results under about 2-300, which can be about 3-10 pages of results depending on what website you are researching through. With a reasonable limitation to what you invest your creativity into, your chances for getting sales and having a successful design rise exponentially.

So then the research becomes a large part of the creative process. You need to be aware of topics and pages that have a passionate following. That includes keeping up with trends and microcosms to provide art for those communities. This could be as simple as watching the news or keeping up with trending hashtags on social media to see which ones are catching fire. If you can preemptively jump into a trend as it is gaining popularity, you will definitely reap the rewards!

Funny memes or recurring jokes can work great. If a short phrase is catching on, sometimes it is enough to just make the design that phrase alone. The minimalist design has its own appeal and has the benefit of of being even easier to make and throw up on the marketplace!

There is no prerequisite to you having any affiliation to the designs. Maybe it's something that you know nothing about but you see the trend growing or overhear a friend mention it. If a potential purchaser looks for that topic on one of the shirt websites, they will not hold out on their purchase until you prove your knowledge and community involvement.

Designing By Importing Designs

You probably picked up this book like many people, wanting to jump into the online game and willing to do whatever it takes. But you may be thinking at this point, "This strategy doesn't apply to me. I'm not an artist or designer!"

Many aren't, but freelancers looking for work are flooding over into the Internet. People who have specific skills to offer and are willing to negotiate a price. This can take the form of sites where you can hire the freelancer for a long term relationship or even as a case by case basis.

Fiverr is an extremely popular website where you can likely find any niche jobs ranging from social media follower boosting to bugging your ex! The site name derives from the lowest price offered for gigs on the site as 5 dollars. There, designers compete amongst each other for paying clients and charge no more than 30 dollars per shirt. You can go lower and still have an amazing design.

Chapter Three: Selling Shirt Designs

However, it's your job to conduct the research and determine which markets are worth your investment before asking your designer to make the design. These highly sought after designers are aware of entrepreneurs who do this strategy and usually include the commercial rights in their contract, so there's no worry involved.

The expense compared to the potential revenue is almost unreal. You enter into one of these sites that sell your shirt design in accordance with the individual purchaser and only pay for a design, assuming you are not capable of making your own. So the one time payment for each design is made to the freelancer and then it goes to work for you generating income!

The sites take a cut of about 5-10 dollars for the manufacturing and shipping and you take home the rest. For a 15-20 dollar shirt, that is about 5-10 dollars per shirt sold. And then those sales can go on autopilot as long as they are in a well-fitted niche!

Chapter Four:

Ebook Publishing

You slowly realize when you enter into the online domain that most businesses still exist online, but with a slight tweak. Publishing has been going through some rocky periods since the inception of the Internet, introducing competition for consumers and ease of reading.

Morphing Markets

This trend is similar to the reduction of magazine subscriptions and the massive growth of people signing up to receive online content in regular intervals. The delivery method is instantaneous and unread content doesn't necessary 'pile up' to be visually unpleasant. People might take their email inbox's cleanliness very seriously, but most don't get uncomfortable with a backlog of unread newsletters in their inbox.

The main advantage physical magazines seem to hold onto is almost their motto "I like holding something in my hands and flipping through it." I would argue that this isn't a preference for most, only a tradition and association that they are uncomfortable breaking. In a few generations from now, I can imagine the opposite will be said. The older generation will

Chapter Five: Becoming An Affiliate

associate read from a screen as the natural state of reading content!

And with the slowdown of magazine subscriptions, those companies have morphed with the market and now offer their entire magazine online to retain relevancy. This move bridges the gap between the remaining population that must read a physical copy and the online consumer that spends the majority of their free time on a screen.

With this huge change in the content we read, it still amazes me that bookstores are still open and surviving. To me, it's like someone selling water in bulky water bottles while across the street they are selling water filters for your home to have water on demand! Granted, bookstores have taken a change of direction as well. The major name bookstores can see the change in market climate and Barnes and Noble has taken note. They have created their own digital reader device called the Nook, all the while still offering the books physically in bookstores and offering a better selection of food and beverages, as well as wi-fi, at their cafes.

Needless to say, this area is very interesting and has insane profit and passive income potential! In a way, you can become your own little bookstore, but you can cut off the physical book aspect and just sell your books digitally.

Taking Action

People like to see books as a far off goal, similar to becoming a musician. It's in the vein of "One day I'll do that." That usually stems from a dangerous standard of perfection that can put your interests on the backburner for year after year. We all want to put out something that we're proud of, but when that desire stretches to putting something in the 'one day I will' category, it actually goes into the 'I will never' category.

Worst-case scenario, you put out a book and it doesn't sell very well. Maybe it gets unfavorable reviews. The best thing you can do is learn from it, then go back and punch it up with more research, taking the reviews into account as free constructive criticism. Even after submitted, your ebook isn't set in stone. If you forgot a crucial piece of information or messed up a page somewhere, it can be easily accessed and updated for previous and future sales.

When people think about writing non-fiction, they think that they aren't smart enough for that. They don't see themselves as an authority on a subject and might be scared that a figure in the genre will strike them down as a phony. These are all self-limiting beliefs. You only hurt yourself by insisting that you can't do it while compiling your case for a self-fulfilling prophecy.

The quicker you say "Why not?", the quicker you march down the road to passive income.

Genre And Focus

You may have your interests and an instant topic you're ready to jump into but I recommend jumping in with a smart direction. The first question is whether you should write about non-fiction or fiction. In my experience, non-fiction is the current market that is most sustainable and easiest way to make money. Selling in fiction tends to be centered more on the weight that your author name holds. An entire brand needs to be built around your name, encouraging the quality of the book.

Chapter Five: Becoming An Affiliate

Building a brand around non-fiction books is beneficial as well but not as crucial. People buy non-fiction books to usually answer a question they have on their mind or get an in depth look at interesting topics. As long as the book's title has the keywords that they were searching for, a purchase is likely to occur!

The current largest platform where you can self publish ebooks is on Amazon's Kindle marketplace. The deal is similar to providing designs for shirts, the site takes a cut of the sale and you get the remaining amount! And like the designs, you need to only provide the ebook document, and Amazon will handle all of the selling details and complications!

This option is revolutionary. Not only were people at once hesitant to write their own book because of the effort required, but also the hassle of finding a publisher to take your book on. Now, as long as your book follows the platform's basic standards of quality, you can throw your book up for sale to millions of people. Right after you insert the last period, you can instantly upload it, reducing your worry solely to the book's quality.

Researching For The Best Ebook

The market research is critical for not going in blind and wasting time and money on a book that doesn't sell a single copy!

Like the shirt design strategy, you type in keyword or topic into the search bar of the ebook site and examine the results. It's best if the results are a few hundred or a couple thousand. Keywords that reach far into the multiple thousands or tens of thousands of results are an ocean where the possibility to getting noticed is close to zero. The topics that you may instinctively look up at first may be in this over saturated category.

The true detective work comes in finding a keyword that has a reasonable amount of results and is of a topic that people are searching for. In reality, this is the most time consuming part of the process, and rightly so! A bad keyword or topic will make all work done afterwards irrelevant.

And a curious thing you may find while doing your research is that the book lengths are shorter than a normal book. On each book page where they show more detailed information, they also may display the page count and you would be surprised to see how many books are under about sixty pages. There are still plenty with hefty page counts like books you would find in a physical bookstore but ones half the size are right next to them in the ebook rankings.

Ebooks have also given birth to an unexpected trend. It's a strange phenomenon but along with the rise of ebooks and ereaders, smaller books are being purchased and aren't criticized for their short length. I believe it's because the people who buy non-fiction online want an ebook to figure something out something quickly.

The purchasers don't mind the shorter books, as long as they get a sufficient amount of information for their purchase. Another theory I have is that when buying a book in a physical bookstore, you pick up the book and evaluate the quality based on the thickness of total pages. Ebooks somewhat pass over that and place more emphasis on the quality and where the author went far enough into the topic for the reader.

This aspect of the ebook marketplace makes the chance to enter even easier! Not only can you publish the books yourself, but also you don't have to write the usual physical book length of one hundred plus pages. The option to do so still remains, but writing a shorter book doesn't nullify your book's success in the ebook market.

Writing The Ebook

Delegation is a much bigger investment for this strategy. Designers are willing to charge about twenty dollars for making a shirt design, but writing an ebook is much more work. Even if you know everything about a topic and are a highly skilled writer, writing it all down will take at least a few days to a week. You may have this time to spend on writing an ebook, and in that case, go for it!

Most will search for writers to delegate so that they can leverage their time for more research and other income opportunities. The same process applies, hiring freelancers, comparing the rates per words they are charging. The spectrum of writer quality here can sway drastically.

A writer with poor writing skills and poor English will be offering their services at a low rate but will require revisions on your part after the product is delivered. And on the other end, you can hire an experienced native English writer with rate that can add up to 500 dollars total for the ebook.

The cheaper writers have the tendency to plagiarize a majority of the book, which delivers the ebook faster but also places the plagiarized book as your responsibility. Software is available to check for blatant plagiarism and even some websites allow you do a basic check on your work for copying.

Judge Your Book By Its Cover

When people search through a list of books, in a bookstore or online, they skim through the covers to see which one pops out at them. This book gets an inspection from the potential buyer and maybe even a sale, or else they pick up the next most eye-catching cover.

Even if your ebook is on the front page for the keyword, its dull cover will push it down to the rankings to being rarely bought. Regardless of the content inside, the cover gets the potential buyer to even give your ebook a chance. The cover may even hold precedent over the content!

With the ease of publishing your own ebook, covers have been slightly overlooked, and you can tell with many ebooks that show up from searches. There are ebooks with images that don't relate well to the keyword. There are titles that are barely readable against background color. Some just are plain ugly!

Freelancers to the rescue! They will make a cover for you, sometimes from just the title alone, while some request an image too. Free images sites are abounding on the Internet but to get an image that really jumps out, you'll want to visit a site that sells pictures. When searching for an image, think to yourself, "If this image was next to the other results that came up on the ebook search, would I click this one?"

You don't need to think too hard about it. Rely on your instincts for which image grabs your attention and also relates to the ebook topic. And if you are really torn between images to choose from, you can have your freelancers make covers for all your chosen images. Most freelancers don't charge much for cover creation since it is just typing out the title onto the

Chapter Five: Becoming An Affiliate

image provided with light font manipulation and pleasing colors.

Chapter Five:

Becoming An Affiliate

Close to everyone has heard the two words 'affiliate marketing' but are they aware of what it actually means? I can admit that I was in the dark at one point, and placed it on a pedestal as an excuse to never dig deeper. It was one of those things that seemed far too complex for a complete newbie to get any headway in.

Finding Affordable Mentorship

But as I have explained before, the Internet is still in its young phase and has massive room for people to continue to join and plant their feet to acquire passive income. And the truth is, while there may be a large number of people online and also working on an affiliate marketing strategy, many are doing so with the wrong mindset.

It is the prevailing idea that everything is a scam that holds many back from embracing the anonymity of the Internet and using it to its fullest potential. It is my belief that those days are long gone. Scammers do not stay around long by the nature of the game they're playing. The Internet has countless blogs that review products, courses, and mentorship and give their honest opinion to not lead their readership astray. A

Chapter Five: Becoming An Affiliate

scammer has a very short life span among the transparency of networking that is the Internet.

This fear of being scammed is mostly bolstered by the media, who take the largest stories, wherever they happen and report on them, as if it was happening to your next-door neighbor. And in recent times, even the media can't find those juicy stories anywhere anymore.

With your barrier lowered and mind ready to learn, you are ready to leverage your learning to fly past those who insist on starting from scratch with inevitable mistakes. There is someone out there who has done exactly what you want to do, and select few of those people are happy to share the knowledge for either personal mentorship or an online course purchase.

This mindset is not to be overlooked. It is the difference between picking up a baseball bat, practicing hitting alone on a tee-ball and hiring a coach who can fast track your success. The online world might seem lonely at times but I assure you, there is ALWAYS someone who has pushed through the obstacle or mistake you may be having at that exact moment.

All this relates to affiliate marketing with the idea that the premise of this chapter is true. Affiliate marketing is not the easiest route to get rolling on, but that also means that the potential profit is huge because of this same reason. People attempt to build an affiliate kingdom from scratch and usually end up scrapping it when time and money invested become too disheartening. Of course this same path is available for you to take but why stumble when you can have a guide for the exact strategy that you want.

These courses or mentors are incredibly thorough, and they expect you to work your butt off if you're serious about applying it. There are hours of video guides with examples and hourly personal video chat coaches if you so desire. And the fear of scamming goes even farther out the window when you see that these mentors are selling through major ecommerce websites that take scamming extremely seriously. If you were legitimately scammed with a faulty product, as long as the payment was through a trusted e-commerce site, the refunds will be promptly dealt with.

Selling Your Recommendations

Affiliate marketing runs along the concept of selling someone else's product for a commission on the sale. In theory, you can do it instantly. Make a video about a product and have the affiliate link in the description, or make a quick website talking about how great a product is with the affiliate link provided. But, once again, smart work takes precedent over fast work.

Many courses and experienced affiliate marketers will show the importance of growing your online presence. This includes taking full advantages of current SEO tactics and examining markets to see which are worth pursuing. With clear focus and consistent work, your presence will grow, allowing for the beginning of affiliate marketing.

As a rule of thumb, you can to stick to selling the products that you have bought yourself, so your endorsement isn't fallacious. If you start affiliate marketing with high priced, low quality products just to get a higher commission on the sale, your reputation will be torn to shreds. People respect transparency and will slowly become invested in you, potentially buying all products you promote.

Chapter Five: Becoming An Affiliate

When you have the correct size to begin affiliate marketing your recommended products, it follow the passive income ethos as only a burst of work for constant income. Maybe one post or video reviewing the product in detail and another about the product from a different angle. And with the strategies of gaining website or video visibility from mentors, all you have to do is let that post sit and get readers.

A Comprehensive View

The beautiful thing about affiliate marketing is the scale you can expand it to. You can follow the advice of a course and get minimal traffic to start getting niche readers and sales with upfront work. But if you want to bring the business further, you can continue to grow your brand and putting your personality out there, involving more and more online marketing skills to build more income.

You will learn about the well of untapped bounty that is email marketing as it relates to affiliate marketing. In short it is the art of gathering leads and keeping them engaged in your value packed periodic emails. This direct contact allows for quick relationships to grow and trust to build, guaranteeing sales for an affiliate link you may put out.

The trust you gain from people also transfers to what products you put out. Those that become loyal to you will feel compelled to buy all products you personally put out. It's like brand loyalty in your favorite restaurant, but with simply with a website and consistent content! The roles will switch and people will be asking to get an affiliate link to your product, putting you in a much more comfortable position.

This can become a beautiful circle of leveraging your work. You will be selling other people's products, possibly your own products, and maybe even getting sales off of others affiliate marketing FOR you!

Truthfully the process of affiliate marketing is a journey and requires learning specific knowledge in many areas so I cannot go deeply into it. The message in this strategy that I'm trying to convey is that if you have the funds to invest, do it. Research for courses, testimonials, understand the money back guarantee period if they have it. Dedicating yourself to something like this upfront is a major step and looking for detailed courses and mentorship has a more underhanded benefit.

You respect what you paid for.

You can buy a book that you like as both a hardcover and paperback. The hardcover usually costs more; let's say that it cost double what the paperback is. Both have the exact same content inside but it's the hard cover's perceived quality derived from the price that makes you give it more respect.

Personal mentorship that costs you thousands per hour will have you super attentive during your talk, taking notes, and getting every question you have out of your system. Compare that with watching a Youtube video on the subject, where you are watching passively and aren't putting weight on the advice they're providing.

Investment adds urgency to the task at hand by adding an extra point of accountability, where you don't want the few hundred dollars you spent on mentorship to go to waste. In the current economy, where people hold onto their money

Chapter Five: Becoming An Affiliate

tighter, this unexpected consequence has the potential to breed more committed workers.

Chapter Six:

Grow Into A Youtube Icon

Your first thought about Youtube is probably that you are not funny or interesting enough. Do you have friends that find you funny and interesting? Making Youtube videos is basically like you are talking to them. Forcing a personality for the sake of the camera wears thin fast, and people become quickly turned off by the lack of authenticity. Your focus should be more on providing immense value for a very tight demographic.

Pursuing Youtube might straddle the line between passive income and active income, although it leans more to something that can be creatively fulfilling when compared to the previous ideas provided.

In the active income sense, you will be uploading videos regularly to keep your channel relevant and gaining more traction in the Youtube algorithm, and they will take more time to edit than a post on an affiliate website. And it is this active aspect that forces you to enter a genre that you have drive to pursue.

Everyone who enters into any new shiny endeavor thinks that the commitment is no big deal. The fresh idea yields a feeling of infinite motivation yet, no matter what you started, you will

Chapter Six: Grow Into A Youtube Icon

eventually feel less interested and loose drive. This is nothing to be scared of. Just something to be aware of.

It is this area that many fall victim to because of the obsession with 'following your passion.' People think that passions hold an endless well of drive when it is not entirely true. I see passions as, accepting that this thing I love now will become difficult, but I love it enough to push through those hard times. And something like Youtube will take more work than other online methods for income, so it needs a bit more internal thought before jumping on a specific vein.

The Passive Income Qualities Of Youtube

Unless you are posting about current events, videos on Youtube don't really have an expiration date. A funny or informative video that is a couple years old can still continue to get views, as well as get shared by a social media personality and go viral.

You are stacking up your videos to grow your view count and passive income potential. The common view about Youtube is that monetization only includes putting ads on your videos, where you get a fraction of a cent per view. If this is the only way you address monetization on your channel, you are going to have virtually no success.

You can throw the strategy of affiliate marketing on virtually anything, and Youtube videos are no different. In whatever genre you focus in on, there are physical or digital products that people are selling and that offer affiliate programs. A small mention in your video or a whole video dedicated to the product and your subscribers will take action from there.

If the product is popular and frequently searched for in Youtube for reviews and testimonials, you have the potential to get a wider scope of potential buyers past your subscribers. Basic video quality standards can propel you to a high rank, but even that's not very strict in the Youtube algorithm. You likely have watched many videos where the guy is holding his phone recording himself. Far from a stringent video budget!

Even if the product itself doesn't have an affiliate program, there's a high chance that Amazon sells it and they have an affiliate program you can sign up for. Just go through a simple questionnaire and you get access to affiliate links to any product you can find there!

This strategy is great for reviews in a genre that you are involved with anyway. Reviewing a movie with a link in the description. Reviewing a book with a link in the description. Reviewing a video game with a link in the description. The ideas can stretch in many directions; it's only advised that you stick to one main area once you begin to gain traction in the Youtube algorithm.

Ads is what most people know of and why most people think Youtube is only useful for those who get millions of views each video, which translates into a few thousand dollars per video. This ignorance only turns into a limiting belief that convinces you to look into other online arenas.

It is true that ads do not hold much merit on their own for a smaller channel, but that's why monetization education is key. Ad revenue can build upon itself with each new video and with no extra work done, that isn't too shabby. It is simply just a facet of the potential on Youtube because in reality, they want to support their channels!

Chapter Six: Grow Into A Youtube Icon

The game is changing with partnering and brand deals as another source of Youtube monetization. As you grow you essentially become digital real estate with your subscriber views that others will pay to partner with and promote themselves.

The major benefit to paid shoutouts and the like is the minimal effort it takes. A simple ten second promo at the end of your video can net you a good sum for only a few more words in your script. This type of partnership takes a bit of networking to gain mutual respect and enough friendliness to take the dive and join forces with another.

The Best Marketing Tool

Even if you don't want to follow any advice on how make money ON Youtube, it should still be used. Any following on Youtube can translate into your own website or sales of products that you may be creating. The majority of people like to consume content through videos as opposed to read a post and these people can be harnessed through Youtube to lead into your site.

You may have a website where you post regularly and have a paid section. It explodes your scope to make a video for every post you make. The process can be made even easier if you read your blog post for the video, so you don't have to worry about concocting a fresh script. You would be astonished to see the extra traffic you get from putting a video on Youtube to go along with every new post you make. Take full advantage of the video content audience.

Chapter Seven:

More Passive Income Avenues

I focused my attention on online methods for the previous strategies because I truly believe them to be the most fruitful, especially with the young age of the Internet. But there are other areas you can look into for passive income that many have known about for some time. The only thing is that the passive income received might not be as significant.

Renting Out Property

This is one that usually flies over most heads for its large learning curve and barrier to entry. However, those that have taken the plunge have sworn by the reward received. Choosing a smart property can guarantee you consistent income for close to no work involved.

Real estate has its own entire bookstore genre so there is only so much I can explain here. The core concept is to understand the importance of the rental property location, take a significant hit with the initial investment, and then keep the property in extraordinary condition to allow for happy paying tenants. Once enough time passes, with a smart investment your payment or loan will be paid back and everything afterwards is passive income!

Chapter Seven: More Passive Income Avenues

It may not seem so sexy because, at first, all your income from the tenants will go to the mortgage payment or recuperation. It's similar to the large investment in a college education for a higher yearly salary to pay it back. And like college, you need to make sure you do your research before jumping in. A good or bad random decision can cost an equal amount of capital but the reward promised is really what matters.

The only real aspect that can translate into reducing the passive income qualities of this strategy is the maintenance of the property for the tenants. If any damage or mishap happens on the property, it becomes your direct responsibility to address the problem immediatly. The more attentive you are to the issues on your property, the happier your tenants will be, allowing room for more success.

However, this can be transferred to the attention of someone else, just like the online tactics. Property managers take this burden on to truly allow rental properties to be a passive source of income. It's at least something to consider before committing to owning a rental property. How involved do you want to be in the maintenance, and are you able/willing to invest even more to delegate the responsibilities out for peace of mind?

A similar vein to renting out property is the recent explosion of temporary room rentals for trips and vacations. Airbnb has become a household name that offers the option to put up a section of your home for rental and allows you to search the area you are traveling to for rooms that destroy the hotel competition. The site consists of people looking to make a bit of extra honest money with their reviews and reputation on the line to hold them accountable.

Of course the success of your listing relies heavily on the location of your home relative to any cities or exciting communities nearby. But even so, there's not much reason to not put up a free room you happen to have in your home on Airbnb or similar sites. If you get a request and purchaser from the site, you have plenty of time to prepare the room beforehand. They won't show up to your door without notice and expect a perfect room.

The extent you go past this is all on your preference. Some people like being left alone on their travels and some will want to get to know you and your family along with a tour of the area. The idea is to not make it too difficult for you or the guy visiting. At the minimum, provide a key and basic rules of the house to follow. Airbnb handles this aspect beautifully putting the specific rules of the room and house in the room listing. This includes bringing pets, smoking inside, extras fee for not cleaning up after yourself, etc. which clearly displays your expectations.

You would be surprised to see what type of listings work on Airbnb. If you are close to a large city, putting up your couch as a room can get people on board, as long as you price your nights accordingly. Backpackers who use Airbnb will likely choose the cheap option anyway because they are traveling for the area's culture and not for a king's night sleep!

Smaller Online Options

Licensing photos has become a popular strategy online to gain a bit of money for something that you do for fun. Bloggers who know how to make their sites engaging for their readers have pictures in all of their posts, to make the read more diverse and interesting. Other applications of using licensed pictures can even expand to creating artwork for books or logos.

Chapter Seven: More Passive Income Avenues

The alternative to people going for licensed photos is free stock photos, which are a major step down in options and quality.

For this strategy, you have to be honest with yourself. When you go somewhere and take beautiful pictures of architecture or nature, what do you end up doing with those pictures? If they have you in the frame you might put them up on social media but otherwise they collect digital dust and just are kept as a memento.

You can still enjoy your photo and put it up for sale on a photo-licensing site for other to use for their creative desires. Using a high quality camera for your pictures is a plus that help for those who want to scale your photo up, allowing for the resolution to not be diminished. However, you shouldn't go out of your way and get a heavy-duty camera just for this strategy. I'm relaying this because in my experience, most adults I come across already own a serious camera to capture family moments.

Another area online with only a minor barrier to entry is the app market. The concept is similar to ebooks in that you create the content and the company you publish it on handles the rest of the details. The company benefits from the variety of options so they make it very friendly for a novice to publish a fresh app.

Apps have their own tactics for monetization, with the use of ads ingame as well as in-game upgrades. With the latter unique tactic, you can sell your app for free but sell extra features once you get the customer hooked in. Apps also benefit from the ebook phenomenon where selling extremely low can be profitable for both the publisher company and the app creator. It knocks more expensive competition out of the park and people are more willing to take a chance with something that is only a few bucks.

Knowledge about coding and marketing would make this a no brainer for you but there are always the very willing freelancers available. The app creation demand has shown itself so there is always someone willing to take your idea on and turn it into reality!

Conclusion

I congratulate you on completing this first step in learning about passive income, so that you too can get closer to a spot of financial freedom and happiness!

No longer will you think that passive income is only something that lucky people attain. It takes hard work and dedication upfront for a reward of making money while you sleep. That sounds like a good deal to me! Once you start seeing the difference of success and failure as simply when you decide to take action, there will be no more excuses available.

This book was a primer to get your feet wet into what passive income options are available and what the Internet can offer. If you are serious about this journey, I URGE you to follow my advice I mentioned earlier about mentors and mastermind groups. Find someone who you admire who is doing what you want and study them. Maybe ask them for coaching and surround yourself with like minded and positive individuals who propel you to where you want to be.

Lastly, if you enjoyed this book, it would be much appreciated if you could leave a review on Amazon. The best way for this book to make its way into the hands of more readers is through truthful reviews about this work. Please write what you liked about this book and what could be improved upon. Any and all feedback is helpful as I continue to serve the needs of my readership.

Thanks and good luck on your journey!

www.ingramcontent.com/pod-product-compliance
Lightning Source LLC
Chambersburg PA
CBHW061229180526
45170CB00003B/1222